I0422070

Peace and Prosperity in our Time?

A discussion of the global financial crisis, risks of hyperinflation, loss of civility, compassion and common sense in modern society and the potential for peace in the world.

By Haywood Roberts

Introduction

The start of the 21st Century has been a tumultuous time both in terms of peace and prosperity. From the internet bubble of the late 20th Century, which collapsed the stock markets in 2000 with the passing of the Y2K concerns, to the attacks on the World Trade Center in 2001 and the financial and housing collapse of 2008 it is no wonder that people are nervous and concerned. Are we doomed to stagnation or worse, leading perhaps to war, famine and the return of the horsemen of the apocalypse as so many fear? While the problems are serious it is not my belief they are beyond solution.

This book is an anthology of articles on some of the issues of peace and prosperity hoping to give insight into what has gone wrong and what has gone right and what is possible in our future.

Whether the new global economy and political order will be able to regain its footing or whether it will slide into deeper and deeper financial and social upheavals will depend in large measure on whether we can return civility to our political dialog and put in place policies so that business can innovate and successfully compete in an increasingly global economy while also reversing the trend to a shrinking, if not disappearing, middle class.

We have come a long way since the Kennedy administration where in his inaugural address John Kennedy asked the question, "Ask not what your country can do for you, but what you can do for your country." Alas, it seems of late that the question has been turned on its head. One commentator has noted that those who vote for a living are now outnumbering those that work for a living. We see almost daily continual attacks on the 1% and the inequality of wealth both in the United States and worldwide. The danger of class warfare is a real one and those stoking the flames of that warfare for political gain may come to regret their polemics. Likewise we have gone from the Kennedy days where we sought out the "best and the brightest" to where we are seemingly teaching to the lowest common denominator in our class rooms and seeking to raise up those at the bottom not by raising them up but by pushing those above them down. Anyone seeking to put the best and the brightest into positions of leadership today are castigated as "elitist" or "racist." Terms used indiscriminately and interchangeably by many who are seeking to promote their own social agenda. So is it any wonder that our economy is in the doldrums and our unemployment, measured accurately, has reached unacceptably high levels?

Solutions to these problems will not be easy nor will the reintroduction of civility into our political discussions. Unfortunately for ratings the media tends to only fan the flames of discord, choosing to focus on the most outrageous or those who can scream the loudest. How very different are the dialogs today than from the founding of the nation or even from the period of the last civil war. And yes, I say last because it is not inconceivable that those fanning the flames today may well engender another civil war that will splinter the United

States into new regional countries much as has happened elsewhere in the world.

So there is much to consider and thoughtful people will have to consider these issues and seek solutions if we are to avoid serious political and economic catastrophes as the 21st Century progresses. The 20th Century saw two of the most horrific world wars and while so far we have avoided repeating those mistakes it is not inconceivable that the foundations of a third are now being laid. One can hope not, but hope alone will not solve the issues confronting us.

This small book will not solve the problems nor will it even provide great insight into solutions but rather it is intended to stimulate discussion of these issues in a way that is hoped thoughtful people will begin to consider what steps are needed to achieve genuine peace and prosperity.

The time is short and the task is enormous. May we, either through luck, or skill, or both, achieve once more a civil society living in harmony and with genuine economic opportunity for all based on their ability.

Table of Contents

Chapter 1 The Financial Crisis, its Causes and the Lessons to be Learned.

As we entered the fall of 2008 we found ourselves dealing with a financial crisis that could, before it is over, equal or exceed that of the 1930's. While conditions have improved since 2008 it is not clear that we have yet avoided the economic Armageddon that this collapse risked. While the future is unknown we can identify the principal causes of this crisis, both immediate causes as well as those buried in the days after World War I. Yes, this crisis has its roots that far back in history.

Before going back to the aftermath of WWI it is useful to identify the genesis of the most recent crisis. That genesis goes back to the days before the S&L crisis of the 1980's. Faced with the costs of the Vietnam War, which was not financed with taxes but by printing money, we entered the 1970's with an inflation the United States had not seen in its modern economic history. After the deflation of the 1930's and until WWII prices had been stable. Even after WWII prices rose at a slow inflationary pace. But by 1970 interest rates and prices were rising rapidly, eventually reaching double digit levels. Part of the cause was the financing of the Vietnam War and part of the cause was the oil embargo of the 1970's. But one result was the deregulation of the financial industry and the birth of the first money market funds. The fears left by the Great Depression of bank failures gave way to fears of the value of savings eroding through inflation. People sought a way to counter inflation that was depleting the value of their dollar. It is ironic indeed that the Reserve Fund, which was at the heart of the immediate crisis, was the first of these money market funds.

While creating money market funds started as a small step it rapidly began to put pressure on banks and savings and loans. Banks and savings and loans had for decades been regulated in what they could pay on deposits. To encourage home ownership the savings and loans were given a one quarter point advantage over the banks but were restricted to making home loans. With the birth of the money market funds the savings and loans saw their deposit base threatened. When deregulation allowed them to compete with banks and money markets few in the industry had any experience in such competition and were ill prepared to deal with it. Often they found they had no place locally to loan the deposits they were generating at profitable rates and so they combined with other savings and loans to buy participations in large loans far flung from their local base. Areas experiencing rapid growth and need for funds. Then oil prices collapsed in Texas and with it the value of Texas real estate. At the time Texas was one of the hottest real estate markets in the country. Even the very best real estate plunged in value. Loans that appeared solid when made were now under water and in work out mode. Management of savings and loans just could not bring themselves to write off the losses. They were in disbelief. Mixed in was a certain amount of greed and fraud, but for the most part it was a combination of badly managed deregulation and bad luck that ended up with the

Resolution Trust Corporation being created to take over the failed industry and sort out its loans.

Moving to the 1990's we saw a dot com mania that was a reminder of past financial bubbles. From the famous tulip bulb mania of the 1700's to the Florida land bubble of the 1920's to a stock market built on borrowed money and speculation that crashed in 1929-1933. It is interesting to note that often these periods seem to follow periods of great upheaval in the form of major wars. Maybe it is in the human psyche to want to feel good after feeling so bad so long. Enthusiasm is perhaps born of despair. Whatever the reason the 1920's were a release from the terrible war to end all wars and a period of great enthusiasm. And the excesses bred by that enthusiasm led to an ultimate collapse.

Following World War II we had another period of enthusiasm. The 1960's saw great excitement over the start of the electronic revolution, from TV to color TV to the computer. The innovations forced on us by war began to be translated into products for the civilian economy. We never experienced the level of euphoria of the 1920's in part because of the Cold War and the threat of nuclear disaster that hung as a dark cloud over the world. World War II ended, but war did not. As with the dot com mania of the 1990's the excitement over the technology of the 1960's too came to a bad end and resulted in a market crash in 1973-75 that in real terms (though not in nominal terms) was as bad as the 1929 crash. Fortunately this crash did not result in a depression. We can only hope to be so lucky this time around.

As the interest rate rise of the 1970's and early 1980's was finally brought under control (along with inflation) the stock market made a spring back from excessive lows in 1982 until the year 2000. This time Y2K and the expenditures to meet that date (front loaded before 2000) set the stage for the dot com collapse of 2000-2003. Mixed in was the war on terrorism that followed September 11, 2001. The Federal Reserve reduction of interest rates to 1% and holding at that level for an extended period of time combined to help start the housing price boom (and current bust) that amplified our financial risks and set us up for our current crisis.

A review of history shows that after a stock market crash people tend to turn to real estate as a "safe" investment. And when real estate crashes they tend to turn back to the stock market. This is a predictable and somewhat rational response. But early success in both markets, real estate and stocks, ultimately gives way to irrational exuberance, in the words of Alan Greenspan. This time a constellation of other events have brought us to the edge of financial disaster. Starting in the 1990's the baby boom generation was beginning to look to its retirement years and this created a need for the pension and profit sharing system to invest increasingly large sums for when the post WWII baby boom generation would eventually retire. But as interest rates wound down they sought more and more ways to generate higher and higher yields. And the financial community and investment bankers were happy to accommodate.

In the "old days" a bank or savings and loan would take in local deposits and make loans to local borrowers for houses. The bankers knew their market and their borrowers. But in the early part of the 21st Century this changed. The syndication was born, along with sophisticated and complicated instruments variously known as CDO and CDS instruments (about which more later). While a single subprime loan might be risky the syndicators convinced the pension plans and other investors that in the modern sophisticated world while a single loan was high risk a collection of such loans were safer. And you could choose a portion of that loan to invest in (the best of the worst) that would make you safer still. The rating agencies were brought in to stamp these with AAA credit standing and give cover to the pension and profit sharing managers who gobbled up these high yielding derivative instruments. And the creators of these loans succumbed to the temptations of making riskier and riskier loans ending with so called liar loans (no documentation and taking the word of borrowers for their income and other collateral with a wink from the mortgage brokers). Since housing prices were going to go up forever they would loan 125% of the current "value" of the home. Appraisers were encouraged to give high valuations and those giving highest values got the most business. No one wanted to look closely at what could go wrong. The naked emperor appeared fully clothed to too many cheering observers. Until the day the cheering stopped.

As more and more cheap money was thrown at housing quickly housing became less and less affordable as people speculated on housing. House flipping became common. Stories abounded about millionaires created over night from borrowing and real estate investing. TV infomercials pushed one get rich quick real estate scheme after another. House prices, like the price of tulip bulbs in an earlier bubble, had no upper limit. They always went up in value so have no fear. No one seemed to connect the dots that this was the same thing that brought the dot com era (and the tulip bulb mania) crashing down.

In an earlier time houses were priced at 2x one wage earner's annual earnings and a loan based on that formula was considered a prudent loan. But in the modern era this quickly rose to 5x. And with two wage earners in a family now common both incomes were used to determine what was affordable. Divorce rates, economic risks and other factors be damned. The bubble continued until real estate reached a level that was unsustainable. And of course greed took over, as it does in all manias. Political pressure to make housing affordable for the poorest Americans through Freddie Mac and Fannie Mae added fuel to the fire with a flood of subprime loans to the least sophisticated of home buyers.

The syndication of loans had another pernicious aspect. The generators of mortgages (the mortgage brokers) sold the loans to syndicators who in turn passed them on around the world to governments, hedge funds, pension and profit sharing plans and others. And since the generators of loans did not have to stand behind them once out of their hands the loans were not their problem once bundled and peddled to buyers who were assured the investment in pools of loans were safe. The brokers had no incentive to make sure the loans were good ones. They pocketed their fee and went on to encourage even more of an orgy of real estate speculation.

All this came crashing down with the subprime mortgage crisis of 2006. Had the damage been contained to subprime the current crisis might never have developed. But subprime defaults finally made all those who held the sophisticated Collateralized Debt Obligations (or CDO's) look at what they really owned. And they did not like what they saw. Quickly the value of those instruments began to decline. And the contagion spread to Alt A (high priced non-prime loans) and even to prime loans. No one knew what they owned or what they were worth. Your house mortgage was no longer owned by the local bank or savings and loan but by China, Russia or some far flung hedge fund. You could not go to someone locally to renegotiate your loan. And with mark to market accounting coming in the aftermath of Enron when the market for CDO's disappeared so did the value of the assets. Even if a loan pool would likely eventually work out at 50% if the market priced it at 10% banks and other holders were forced to value these loans at 10%. It was that write off that the $700 billion Paulson plan is intended to address.

Added to the CDO crisis was the CDS crisis. Together all these "derivative" instruments are said to be valued from $455 to 1300 Trillion. Truly staggering sums! CDS stands for credit default swap. It is generated to guarantee a borrower that if the company or country they have loaned money to should default then the counterparty will make good the loss. Which is fine until the counterparty disappears in the magic of bankruptcy which becomes more and more likely as few and fewer assets were kept on the books to back the CDO/CDS market and, when marked to market, even those assets started to disappear.

As the crisis deepened we saw more and more CDS issues marked down severely on the slightest rumor. One event in early October 2008 involved GE, then the world's largest company, which found its CDS spreads threatened which in turn threatened its AAA status. As a result it had to turn to Warren Buffett for a bailout. Before that it was AIG and Bear, Stearns and forced sales of Merrill Lynch, Washington Mutual, Wachovia, etc. Then came Lehman Brothers. Criticized for favoring Wall Street over Main Street the Treasury decided to draw a line in the sand. They chose to let Lehman fail. But they knew not what they wrought! Indeed in recent revelations in 2014 it was clear that the Federal Reserve had no idea the damage they were about to unleash on the economy.

The almost immediate effect of the Lehman collapse was that the oldest money market fund, -- one of the biggest with $64 billion in assets and millions of holders-- faced a run by its institutional holders and was forced to stop redemptions. Millions of holders found their funds frozen. What they thought were safe cash holdings were no longer available for any purpose. Even companies were threatened. When Goodyear Tire and Rubber found that half its working capital cash was now frozen in Reserve Fund it drew down on its bank lines of credit to tide it over. It did not take but a few days for the big holders of cash in prime money market funds to withdraw and put their money into treasury funds or other safe assets. The commercial paper market which relied heavily on the money market funds and already hurt by the subprime and CDO crisis (since many of these funds had holdings of asset backed securities) had to scramble not to follow Reserve out of business. The result was a total freeze of the commercial paper market. A market on which many industries relied to operate. Many of these businesses found they had no place to turn. Big businesses with bank lines of credit drew down their lines of credit (General Motors and Goodyear being just two) making it even more difficult for banks to pick up the slack left by the commercial paper backed money market funds. Those making withdrawals were for the most part institutions that could not put money in banks without risking loss since their deposits in full were not covered by FDIC. So the banks did not benefit from the withdrawals from money market funds. Liquidity in the bank and commercial paper markets dried up almost overnight.

In 2008 businesses around the country were quickly running into trouble and closing their doors and releasing their workers. The largest Chevrolet dealer in the US out of Atlanta, GA operating numerous dealerships in five states declared bankruptcy and put 2700 people out of work because it could not get financing. And rumors were rife. Harry Reid on the floor of the Senate remarked that he knew of a major, and well known, insurance company that was close to bankruptcy. Not mentioning the name the result was a panic in the CDS market for all insurance companies and stocks of Met life and others dropped by a third immediately. In this panic it was sell first and ask questions later!

Meanwhile Congress fiddled with the Paulson plan while the economy of the United States suffered what Warren Buffett has likened to a heart attack. Urging action he said that as the patient is suffering a heart attack it is not time to chastise him for being overweight and having high fat in his arteries.

To sell their plan Paulson, Bernanke and Bush alarmed the entire country (the political equivalent of yelling "fire" in a crowded theater) that we were headed for another depression. Once this ball has gotten rolling downhill it is almost impossible to stop. Words hurt and those used to "sell" the plan to Congress not only failed to achieve the desired result (quick passage of the bill) but caused far more harm than the $700 billion plan would do good by helping to erode even further public confidence. And the Obama administration carried this a step further with another stimulus that once more failed in its objective. Not only were there no shovel ready projects as Obama promised but the benefits went to many who did not need them and not enough to those that did.

At this point we can only watch the forest fire rage and hope it will burn itself out before doing too much long term damage. While since 2009 there has been a painfully slow recovery we are far from out of the woods. The Federal Reserve Quantitative Easing program (QE) has yet to be unwound and the initial steps to unwind this program has already caused serious problems in emerging markets. In this country we have a bloated student loan program that is a major risk. In a political world dominated by special interest lobbies, anti-elitism, democratization and political correctness we have sadly replaced John Kennedy's "best and the brightest" with what often appears to be the "worst and the weakest." If anyone had any doubt they needed only to listen to the Congressional hearings on the Paulson plan. Painful and embarrassing are two words to describe the sad state of those hearings. If a camel is a horse designed by a committee then these hearings prove that a camel with its head where its tail should be is a horse designed by a Congressional committee. And Congress has no compunction about changing the rules in the middle of the game if it is to their political advantage. You may recall that when it was started Social Security was not taxable. Congress in 1983 decided in its wisdom that it was going to tax 50% of Social Security benefits for what it considered higher income seniors. Of course it did not exempt those already retired and who relied on the old system of non-taxation. Nor did it link the breakpoints to inflation guaranteeing (as it did with the Alternative Minimum Tax originally aimed at millionaires) that with inflation soon nearly all seniors would be subject to tax. The argument at the time was that half of social security had never been taxed. Had the new rules applied only going forward and not retroactively this might have been fair. But then ten years later in 1993 it was decided to raise the taxable amount of Social Security to 85% and this time they did not even attempt to come up with a rational explanation….just give us the money! To paraphrase language on our national currency, "In God We Trust…Because We Cannot Trust Congress!" Or for that matter the White House. In a crisis it is every man and woman for themselves!

If there is one lesson to be learned it is the one the prior manias have taught us, from the Dutch tulip bulb boom and bust to the South Sea Bubble to the more recent internet bubble and now the housing and financial bubble. That lesson is that regulation will not trump human nature. Waves of enthusiasm occur and the results are not pretty. One concern coming out of this crisis is the risk of overregulation especially as it affects start up and small business. Over the years I have engaged in small business enterprises but many more I never started due to the cost and concern over excessive regulation and paperwork. Our legal system alone is so burdened with laws and regulations that even the most law abiding risks running afoul of some obscure regulation. We risk aborting small business before it even reaches the marketplace. Fortunately for our economy many budding small business owners do not know the dangers they face and proceed with development of new enterprises unaware of their risk taking beyond the risk of business itself. But how many more throw up their hands in frustration or fear and simply never get started? That we will never know but it certainly is not helping our employment or growth rates in the United States. Of course we need regulation and oversight, no one would argue otherwise. But it has to be easy to understand and comply with and applied with common sense. Whether it be OSHA, EPA, IRS or any of the other three and four letter acronyms that dot our regulatory landscape.

Another area that is currently a major drag on our economy is our health care system. Without getting into a discussion of The Affordable Care Act (more commonly known as Obamacare), about which so much has been written and more will be written, this debate has obscured the out of control costs of health care. In a recent *Time Magazine* article by Steve Brill in the March 4, 2013 edition it was noted that Hurricane Sandy is estimated to cost some $60 billion. While that number is staggering it is only **one week** of the cost of health care. And the United States spends more on health care than the ten next largest countries combined, including Japan, Germany, France, China, the United Kingdom, Italy, Canada. Brazil. Spain and Australia. The article notes we spend more on artificial knees and hips than what Hollywood collects at the box office. And as a percent of GDP the cost of health care is staggering. It was estimated in 2011 to be over 17%. And the Brookings Institute has estimated with the aging of population that it will continue to grow at 1.2% over GDP growth for several decades reaching 25% in 2020. While it is dangerous to project trends into the future if the past is prologue where health care is concerned it is already reaching a point where it is a major economic drag on the economy. Whatever your position on Obamacare there is no question that control of health care costs in the United States needs to be a major priority.

We have survived crises before and we will likely survive this one too. Writing this in 2014 it is still too early to tell the outcome. Many think we are seeing a recovery in the economy but their predictions may turn out to be only wishful thinking. Time will tell. But the pain and suffering of the American people and of people around the world has already been and is likely to continue to be great indeed. Maybe we will learn from the mistakes that have led us here. One can only hope. But if the past is prologue then the prospects of our having learned our lessons is dim indeed. The good news is that all crises pass in time as will this one. But it may be a long and painful process.

Chapter 2. Is Hyperinflation Possible in the United States?

One of the concerns coming out of the financial crisis is that between the Federal Reserve keeping interest rates artificially low for a significant period, its quantitative easing program which has mushroomed the balance sheet of the Federal Reserve, and the large stimulus programs put in place by the Bush and Obama administrations the United States runs the risk of serious inflation or even hyperinflation.

So far so good but we are in the early innings of a long term ball game. At some point interest rates will rise either because the Federal Reserve acts or because bond buyers and lenders insist. So far that has not happened. Gold is often a harbinger of inflation and while it rose in the early stages of the crisis for the last two years it has pulled back significantly. It is doubtful that gold is actually a good hedge against inflation or hyperinflation but whether it is or not it remains a useful barometer of fear. TIPS or Treasury Inflation Protected Securities are perhaps a better indicator of inflation risk. Once more, so far, these have remained quiescent. Does that mean the inflation fear is over? Hardly. Only that the day of reckoning has been postponed. The can has been kicked down the road. Look at Greece if you want a poster child for this sort of problem.

Inflation is one thing. Hyperinflation is another breed of cat altogether. While it is unlikely this will happen in the United States anyone with assets needs to consider the possibility and be prepared to act quickly should this genie pop out of its bottle.

I have been considering the possibility of hyperinflation here in the US. Not just since 2007 but since the 1970's. My conclusion was that the period we are entering was then (and is now) the most likely time for this to happen. With the introduction of unlimited QE by the Fed and the near doubling of the US federal debt in four years (from 10 trillion to 16 trillion) reaching and soon to exceed 100% of US GDP this is no longer a speculative exercise. I am not predicting this occurring, but the risk of it occurring is rising rather dramatically and is worth thinking about and doing sensible planning, to extent that is possible. And the risk of something short of hyperinflation but still significant inflation (10-25% a year) is very possible. If and when this starts there will be very little time to act so some forethought is important.

Below you will find a link to an 11 page report of the Dallas Federal Reserve on hyperinflation focused on the Zimbabwe occurrence 2007-09 but also covering past hyperinflation periods with references to further reading. If you read nothing else on the risk of hyperinflation this is very well worth reading to get a feel for hyperinflation conditions. http://www.dallasfed.org/assets/documents/inst itute/annual/2011/annual11b.pdf

Recently I picked up from the Learning Company's Great Courses series their 12 lectures on Hitler's Empire. I wanted to see if there were things that I did not know about how Hitler went from an unknown to complete dictatorship in 10 years (1922 to 1932). With the Golden Dawn party (Nazi party) in Greece having grown from 2% to 20% support in just a few months of unrest, understanding how this can happen is not just an historical exercise. While I knew much of the history I must say this is one of the better and more useful of the Great Courses series. I thought I knew a lot about the period but have learned a great deal I did not know. Especially about the German hyperinflation of 1923. I knew it grew out of WWI but if I knew the details I had forgotten them. Here is story in nutshell.

After the German unconditional surrender in 1918 they signed a blank check to pay reparations to France, England and Belgium (and they in turn to the US). The amount of reparations were never set forth and when the victors insisted on payment Germany resisted. France finally was fed up and they invaded the Ruhr and seized German industry. Germany in turn called on workers to resist by slowdowns and not working and agreed to pay their wages. They ran the printing presses to pay the workers. Before the invasion the US dollar would buy 4 German marks. Within two years it went to 75 marks in 1921 but really took off in 1923 starting the year at 7,000 marks to the US dollar finally reaching over 4 Trillion marks to the US dollar mid-November. Workers were paid three times a day. They would give their paper money to family members who would quickly buy food for lunch because by lunch those marks were worthless. Draconian economic measures followed which stabilized the economy from 1923 to 1928. Industry was able to protect itself dealing in foreign currencies but middle class savings not in hard assets were mostly wiped out in 1921-22 but totally obliterated and made worthless by November of 1923.

:

Date	Marks	U.S. Dollars
1919	4.2	1
1921	75	1
1922	400	1
Jan. 1923	7,000	1
Jul. 1923	160,000	1
Aug. 1923	1,000,000	1
Nov. 1, 1923	1,300,000,000	1
Nov. 15, 1923	1,300,000,000,000	1
Nov. 16, 1923	4,200,000,000,000	1

The point is that if hyperinflation sets in it can spin so rapidly out of control that it is too late to try and protect assets. Of course right now those who fear this outcome are urging holding gold and silver and while perhaps useful as diversified approach it is probably a flawed strategy. Those promoting gold seem to forget that the US government confiscated all private gold early in the depression. Land is of course a possibility but one has to consider the effects of taxation (and how those taxes can be paid in hyper inflationary period). Diamonds a possibility but not easily divisible. Tradeable items such as long lasting food supplies, etc. an option but a bit hard to protect in any sizeable amounts. And of course any plan can come apart depending on unraveling of social conditions.

This is hardly the only example of hyperinflation. One of the worst is even more recent case in what was once known as Southern Rhodesia. Now known as Zimbabwe they seized farms from white farmers and redistributed them to black natives just at the time of a drought with disastrous results for the agricultural economy. From a stable economy they went to printing trillions of Zimbabwe dollars with the coup de grace coming with issuance of the 100 Trillion Zimbabwe dollar note shown below, the largest denomination note ever printed --- up to now at least. The study from the Dallas Federal Reserve analyzes the collapse of the Zimbabwe dollar ending with the issuance of the 100 Trillion dollar note. http://www.dallasfed.org/assets/documents/institute/annual/2011/annual11b.pdf

As with Germany the currency collapsed in less than a year (2007-08) and ultimately was replaced with stable foreign currencies. Note in particular the chart on page two of the Dallas Fed study showing how rapidly this spiraled out of control, just as it did in Germany in 1923. There are many examples of hyperinflation through the decades including Hungary, Argentina and a host of other countries. The table on page 11 of the Dallas Fed report shows a list of other modern era countries and their rates of hyperinflation. Hyperinflation being defined as a rise in prices more than 50% in a single month.

Reading the Dallas Fed article is well worthwhile to understand roots and causes of hyperinflation in modern society. Of course even the Romans engaged in the practice of debasing their currency by "clipping" their coinage reducing the value of metal coins. But they were not good at leaving charts behind showing the degree of their devaluation. Notes at the end of the Federal Reserve article gives reference for further reading on the subject. While the last year of hyperinflation shows spectacular collapse for those holding a currency about to hyper inflate these become virtually worthless long before the final death spiral. So identifying the incipient signs of hyperinflation are important to those who hold currency assets.

Love the imagery of the Zimbabwe 100 Trillion notes. On face appears what can only be described as being between rock and hard place (or maybe being pressed to death by weight of currency needed to buy loaf of bread?) and on back your choice of going over Victoria Falls or being gored by a water buffalo.

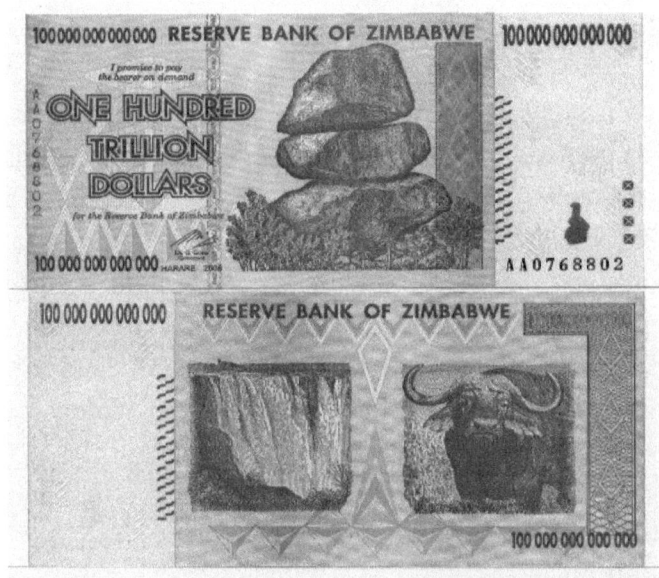

And Germany and Zimbabwe are not even the worst examples of hyperinflation. That honor belongs to Hungary in 1945 where inflation rose in one month to a staggering 1.295x10 to the 16th power!

Hmmm the property I am considering buying in Belize or the Fiji islands may not be so farfetched after all! And that castle in Ireland looking good too (can always pour burning currency down from the ramparts to stave off invaders!). Seriously, I am giving more thought to this and have not yet come to many firm conclusions. But I do think that as farfetched as this might seem it is something to consider. Even if we escape hyperinflation and have high inflation the damage can be severe.

I do think that the following makes certain amount of sense.

1. Having a pantry of food supplies sufficient for three to six months or more in event of serious disruption of the food supply. This is not a bad idea in any case for a variety of potential problems from ice storms to other natural disasters that might disrupt food distribution. You might get tired of ramen noodles and other long lasting supplies but it could be important to have on hand. Fuel is harder to store, especially for long periods, even if you use a fuel stabilizer but at start of trouble having 10-20 gallons stabilized a good precaution as well as not letting tank get below 3/4 full. Same with propane for cooking on grill. Containers for water filled in case water supply cut

off. Vessels for collecting rain water. Need not only for cooking and drinking but also for toilets. As the risk of cyber-attacks on banks and power grid, etc. rises this is another reason to engage in some sensible precautions. Supplies of toilet paper and other personal supply items could be important -- humorous but not so funny really to see sign in the Dallas Fed report saying what not to use in toilets, one item being Zimbabwe dollars!

2. Holding certain amounts of cash, gold and silver but not in any substantial amounts. Just enough in case of banking disruptions. Chances of this being really useful for any extended period I think slim. Same with diamonds and other such stores of value. One thing those recommending gold seem to forget is that in the 1930's people were required to turn in their gold for currency. When things unravel it is hard to tell what governments will do. If you want a recent example see what happened in Cyprus when banks were closed and the Eurozone decided not to honor its equivalent of FDIC protection. While it relented it shows how far governments or quasi governments in the case of the Euro will go in crisis. Same with foreign currencies which under Nixon were subject to exchange controls and in 2014 the Argentine dollar which also saw a collapse and then imposition of exchange controls. Second guessing ahead of time what will work and what not is not an easy task and one is as likely to guess wrong as right.

3. Means of protection in event of serious social disruptions. Difficult to predict or implement but pepper

spray on hand not bad idea and perhaps more. A well-stocked medicine cabinet likely a must as well since social unrest and other conditions may lead to a rise in disease.

4. Plan for relocation to safer areas if necessary and means to get there e.g., fuel. Getting from point A to B when need is obvious, however, travel may be difficult if not impossible and joining with neighbors to protect your area may be wiser course. A bicycle may also prove valuable. Likely better staying put than trying to get to a safe haven but circumstances could dictate otherwise. It is clearly impossible to predict the course of social disruptions.

5. While fixed debts will be wiped out in hyperinflation there is no certainty that hyperinflation will in fact occur but if it does within a year want to pay off any mortgage or other fixed debts with hyper inflated currency before it is stopped and conditions reset. It is possible that despite the running of presses that a severe deflation could occur without preceding hyperinflation. In which case debts are not a good thing! Of course the greatest fear is hyperinflation followed by severe deflation as occurred in Germany after 1929 - hyperinflation in 1923 and deflation in 1930 through the Great Depression. Land could be good investment, especially agricultural, but of course taxes and cost of goods to grow things will skyrocket and with currency worthless having means to pay for taxes, etc. could be a real problem. If land is not near you getting there issue too. And government seizure or control of land is always possibility. As noted before no one can guess what governments will try to do in these circumstances.

6. Holding foreign currency an option but problem is which currency. Swiss francs? Canadian Loonies? Australian dollars? And in times of stress currency controls are almost a certainty. So this is not a likely a useful solution for the average person.

7. Diversification is probably the best chance of success for 401(k) and stocks with stocks held in companies that hold real assets like oil and other commodities and needed items vs. frills. But many companies will be wiped out and it will be hard to tell which. Look at what happened in 2007-8. Not to mention the Great Depression. Many companies that appeared solid disappeared. TIPS a possible option but no guarantee in severe conditions government will honor those commitments. An excellent book on this subject is _Keynes Way to Wealth_ by John Wasik. This is NOT a book about Keynes the economist but Keynes the investor and what he learned (and what nearly bankrupted him) in the Great Depression and then during the war years of WWII. It is a book worth reading. Whether you agree with Keynesian economics or not and whether you are a fan of the New York Times (for whom Wasik writes) you should not be deterred from reading this book.

8. Being prepared to move from cash assets into some form of hard assets very quickly and perhaps TIPS at very first signs of hyperinflation. Savings and bank accounts would be wiped out in less than a year in event of start of hyperinflation but some cash will be needed to pay bills for

utilities, etc. until they run out of sight. Step one would be to buy up quickly food, fuel, toilet paper and other paper goods and any other supplies that are used in daily life and which could quickly disappear. Of course stock piling a certain amount now makes sense. Anti-hoarding laws could be likely so advance planning important but not going crazy about it makes sense. As does keeping your own counsel about what you are doing. Of course once everyone realizes the situation is out of control it is too late to take action. We see this in minor form when people clean out grocery stores, etc. when a hurricane is coming.

These are hard things to think about. None of us wants to think this could really happen. But, the penalty for not thinking about this possibility could be severe.

I am planning to spend more time thinking about this and considering approaches that could make sense in one of three environments: 1) hyperinflation 2) hyperinflation followed by depression/deflation in some form and 3) depression/deflation not preceded by hyperinflation as well as conditions in between like high but not hyperinflation and the 1970's bugaboo - stagflation. Of course always remembering the old joke, "Want to make God laugh, show him someone who plans!"

Chapter 3 The Dumbing Down of America

It is always a mistake to try to simplify complex issues and come to conclusions that may turn out to be logically false. With that in mind one of the issues to be discussed in this book has serious social and economic consequences that unless addressed can doom America to stagnation and to a second class status in the world with much misery and unhappiness within its population. We face numerous serious issues and while this issue is only one of these it does need to be addressed as it permeates society and affects adversely the solution of other major issues.

It was recently 50 years November that President John Kennedy was killed in Dallas to the shock of the world. Many of us remember the Camelot era that Kennedy brought into Washington, DC. Even those of us who were not Kennedy fans or supporters had to admire some of his rhetoric and ideas. In his inauguration speech he had a line quoted often, "Ask not what your country can do for you, but what you can do for your country." A book written about the Camelot era was entitled "The Best and the Brightest" highlighting the effort of Kennedy to fill his administration with the very best and brightest individuals. Contrast that to today when there is attack after attack in the media on what they have termed "Elitism" and emphasis on promoting minority interests and savage results for those who might dare to raise a complaint on matters of policy. Those that disagree with any policy of the Obama administration are castigated as "racist" no matter how far the policy issue is from any racial issue. As one who marched in the South in support of civil rights in the 1960's I find it sad that what we tried to achieve back then has turned into a very ugly attack on free speech and the real equality that we sought to achieve. At least for me the issue was one of right and wrong and an attempt to give everyone in America a fair chance at the American Dream. We have sadly deviated badly from providing opportunity equality to an era of promoting those who are less capable than others merely because of their diversity.

And just to be clear, there is no doubt that there remains undercurrents of real racism but just as the boy crying wolf those who see racism under every rock do themselves and their race a disservice. While I have my reservations about affirmative action both in education and in the workplace I also recognize that there is some need for a level playing field. But just at black athletes would be upset if there were quotas for non-black athletes who cannot perform at high levels just because of their race or color, be it white, yellow or brown, there is the same concern in education and the workplace where affirmative action is employed. Do I know the answer? No. But I do know that in the long run we are not helping those we in the 1960's hoped to help by putting people in positions either in the classroom or the workplace where they are "given" positions not because of their ability or aptitude but because solely of their race. Common sense is required here along with cultivating a culture of both toleration and of encouragement of all students and employees to be the best they can be for their own advancement. It does nothing for self-worth and self-confidence to give grades or jobs to those who are not qualified to perform. Indeed it only raises antagonism and resentment among those not so favored and in the end does not achieve the goal of genuine advancement. And it is worth remembering it is not just race that is a problem here. Those who are obese, unattractive, disabled, older or those who have been out of the workforce raising children, all of these have their problems in the workplace no matter how capable they may be. Law and regulation can only go so far in providing a level playing field for all those who suffer under disadvantages. What is the answer? I wish I knew. But I firmly believe that a recognition of the problem is the first step. I only urge those that seek to remedy the problem by quotas or other measures to consider carefully whether they are solving a problem or merely creating one that may prove even more intractable.

Not long ago I wrote a history of my preparatory high school and in the process noted just how much education has changed since the 1950's. At that time there were few electives and a core curriculum that focused on language, mathematics and science. Looking back at the early days in the 1800's very little had changed except eliminating ancient Greek as a language requirement. Today sadly and in part because of social issues the curriculum is filled with classes that result in watering down of a curriculum. Today there is a tendency to teach to the lowest common denominator rather than seeking to raise up those at the bottom. True there are advanced placement courses for those who qualify by their test scores but this too tends to separate all others in the academic herd. My late wife was a lifelong educator and I was able to see her concern with students receiving less than adequate education. We have some fine schools and fine educators but taking the country as a whole we fall far short of the education provided students in decades past and with countries with whom these students will be competing.

Despite effort to improve education sadly those with college degrees today have seldom a much better education than those with high school degrees in the period before the 1960's, and at much greater expense. And to have an equivalent to what was then a college education today one requires in many cases at least a master's degree if not a Ph.D. It is beyond the scope of this chapter to do other than point out the decline in educational standards and dilution of curriculum. The solution may lie in a required core curriculum with minimum standards and not simply passing along to the next grade those who fail to meet those standards. But the fault lies not entirely with the educational system. Today due to advances in technology there are many more distractions for students than in the past. Cell phones, internet, Facebook, tablets, gaming and a host of other distractions. With two parents working and many single parent homes the ability of the most conscientious adults to guide their young is difficult and in many cases nearly impossible.

The impact of technology on education, be it kids on their smart phones, gaming or e reading cannot be underestimated. Technology has been great for society in many ways but it would be foolish to ignore its drawbacks. I am reminded of a bookmark passed down to me with the saying, "Books should be like friends, few and well chosen." This quote by Samuel Johnson rings as true today as it did in the 18th Century. I worry that with the mind numbing plethora of reading material on the web, e readers, etc. that we are losing focus on selectivity. And that applies in the classroom. Don't misunderstand me. I am a great user and fan of computers, I Pads, e readers and other technological advances. But I also see the problems. To me they are tools to be used where they fit the need but also not using them where there are better alternatives. A recent article in *Scientific American*, November 2013, discusses the downside of e readers. Again, not as a diatribe against them but pointing out the eye strain, the fact that e reading is slower than paper book reading, does not lend itself to the same degree of comprehension and other disadvantages. My son, a university professor, tells me that his students invariably buy their books in paper form rather than e reading form. While they are members of the digital generation they seem to have figured out that their technology has limitations and that paper books have a solid place in their educational experience. I assume they have found, as the *Scientific American* article and its studies cited suggest, that they learn faster and better from paper books than from e reading. But there is a whole industry pushing technology into the classroom and one Texas library recently eliminated paper books in favor of only electronic media. And many schools now either distribute or require students to have laptops, I Pads, etc. as part of their educational experience. This is fine just so long as it does not replace genuine learning and so that it does not contribute to the dumbing down of students.

While calculators have been a valuable aid for many of us there is concern that many students are unable to do even simple mathematics without the aid of a calculator. How many times I have been checking out of a restaurant or store where the cash register has malfunctioned only to see the clerks in panic as to how to do the simple math needed to check out a customer.

Another area of concern is the push to on line education. So far the experience of on line courses has been disappointing. Very few finish their courses and of those that do only some 15% earn high grades. And in some cases the degrees received may look good on an office wall but fall far short of an equivalent campus education. The degrees are often cheap in quality as they are in cost. But as the cost of higher education continues to escalate there is a strong temptation to see this as a panacea and the technology industry is ready to oblige. But as with e readers the on line education does not seem to work except for rare cases of highly motivated students seeking a course they cannot obtain otherwise. Perhaps in the large university where 300 plus are packed into classes those students may get as much or more out of on line courses as they would in the classroom. But I have my doubts even there. There is more to education than simply obtaining knowledge. The one on one experience with a professor and with other students can be invaluable as can the encouragement and giving of direction to students by caring professors. Discussions and talk over coffee often add as much to education as classroom participation. Not to mention all the other aspects of student life on a campus that is missing in an on line course. As with e readers these courses have their place but as a substitute for class room education I have serious doubts and reservations. As a member of Phi Beta Kappa and having graduated from a liberal arts college I am a strong believer in liberal arts education as forming the basis of a solid background for whatever a student later chooses to do in life. I recognize the trend today to more job oriented education but I fear that such a narrow focus does not well prepare many students for life. Learning is, or should be, a lifelong process where curiosity, creativity and joy of learning is a continuous part of an adult experience. I can only hope we learn that while technology can benefit us it can also hinder our development of the skills needed for living a quality life.

Let me be clear, I continue to support the advances in technology as well as giving of equal opportunity to all Americans and indeed to all peoples of the world as well. But with technology we need to understand its best uses as well as its worst uses. And equal opportunity does not mean making everyone equal, only giving them the opportunity equally to achieve success and to advance themselves and therefore the country and the world. And to have that opportunity they must have a quality education that prepares them for being successful in their lives. That is true whether they choose or are capable of a college education or instead learn a trade which will make them productive members of society. We must value those with trades as much as we do those with higher levels of education. Nor should we encourage obtaining degrees simply to obtain a degree.

We should continue to seek the best and the brightest to both advance and lead this country into the future, whether in government or business. Attacking the successful and those that work hard to achieve success out of some warped sense of political correctness does real damage to the country and to those who many of us sought to help with our efforts to achieve genuine civil rights. We need to distinguish between those seeking a hand up and those who are only seeking a hand out.

Chapter 4. The Loss of Civility and Compassion in America

The American Dream of improving economic life for each generation is threatened by many aspects of modern life. And this is not just an American dream but one which resonates around the world.

Among the threats to this dream is a loss of civility, compassion and common sense. The goal of advancing the best and the brightest to positions of leadership has been replaced by a dumbing down of America. Now extolling the best and brightest is labeled "elitism" and degraded. The rise of road rage, school and postal shootings which has generated its own term "going postal" is just one example of decline of civility. As for compassion, our courts either throw the book at someone for a minor crime or let heinous criminals off with light sentences or early parole. Our laws have become so complex that almost anyone can be found to have run afoul of them and that leads to less respect for law. Fear of offending someone is a threat to our freedom of speech and assembly. There is no freedom of speech today in major media for those who do not abide by their code of political correctness. Common sense is thrown out the window in these circumstances. It is the purpose of this chapter to explore briefly what has happened to cause this loss of civility, compassion and common sense and what, if anything, can be done to change the trends in America that threatens its future.

Sadly the terms "racist" and "elitist" have become the 21st century equivalent of being labeled an adulterer in the middle ages or a communist in the 1950's. In the 1950 McCarthy era being labeled a communist or a communist sympathizer resulted in the same black listing as someone who today makes the most mundane statement that offends the prevailing code of political correctness. A corrosive and potentially explosive atmosphere and certainly not one designed to heal wounds of those political correctness seeks to advantage. And corporate America will quickly fall into line for fear of offense and its backlash on their businesses. In light of experience it is hard to blame them. In such an atmosphere meaningful dialog becomes impossible.

Make no mistake. It is not the purpose of this book to defend the comments of those who make offensive statements. But the lack of compassion, much less forgiveness, of offhand comments and the destruction of those deemed offenders threatens and stifles free speech in America. And it drives underground many who would benefit from an open and frank discussion of the issues. Also the risk of using race as an offensive weapon by playing the race card is dangerous precedent. Fanning flames of racial hatred on either side of the issue presents a grave danger to the republic beyond merely the danger to free speech.

In our Congress we see almost daily not just political juggling but virulent attacks on those who disagree with one another. Perhaps this is inevitable but it has not always been so. There seems to be no restraint in speech or action and this as much as election results has resulted in the deep divide inside the Beltway on numerous issues of importance to the United States. Unfortunately 24 hour news and the sound bite has encouraged those who make the most outrageous comments that garner ratings for the networks no matter how much harm they may do.

Returning civility, compassion and common sense to our politics, airways and daily life will only happen if we recognize the problem and begin to deal with it. We need to each consider carefully our words and actions and then hold to account those that do not, one individual at a time. But not at the expense of free speech or without civility, compassion and common sense.

Chapter 5. Thinking the Unthinkable – Splintering of the United States into New and Smaller Countries.

With the 150 year anniversary of the U.S. Civil War occurring early in this decade it seems a propitious time to revisit the issue whether the Union will continue to survive intact or will it be again dissolved. With the continuing inability of Washington to come to grips with serious issues, what was once unthinkable may require a fresh evaluation.

We have seen other nations go through such a process from Yugoslavia and other Eastern European nations splitting into ethnic separate countries to Quebec wanting to leave Canada. Now Scotland is seeking to separate itself from Great Britain and if it succeeds can Wales be far behind?

With increasing pressures of Hispanics, some of whom have an objective of separating California and much of the southwest into either a separate country or to become again part of Mexico, the danger of separation of regions of what is now the United States into separate countries needs to receive serious thought. There have been recent nascent movements toward this goal most recently from conservatives in Texas. But unless we can return civility, compassion and common sense to our political discourse the path to separation is one that may gather more and more momentum as the 21st Century progresses.

It is not the purpose of this chapter to encourage such separation, to the contrary it is a warning that what was once unthinkable is being thought about and could become a reality. We can only prevent the tearing of the United States asunder by restoring its economy and creating an atmosphere of civility in our private and public discourse. The more raucous the dialog the more the risk to creating a divide that can perhaps only be healed by separating into regions or nations with more of a commonality of interest than the United States as a whole.

To think this cannot happen is to ignore history, especially the history of the world after World War II when the great powers that had built colonial empires found those empires dissolving. India going its own way, Africa its own way and the nations of Eastern Europe splintering into homogeneous (or at least more homogeneous) ethnic and religious nations such as in Yugoslavia or the breakup of the Soviet Union. Since World War II there has been no instance of nation states joining together in a new larger political union with perhaps the exception of the Eurozone but in that case (fragile as it appears at the moment) it is an economic union and not a political union.

What form the new nations created out of the current United States might take is only speculative as it will depend as much on economic as political factors. In light of political differences it is not difficult to see the South once again seeking its independence and perhaps the southwest as well. The Midwest too could see itself separating into a more homogeneous union of states. While all of this is currently unthinkable and speculative the seeds of disunion are certainly being sowed and the more our society dissolves into discord, economic stagnation and breakdown of civility can separation fever be far behind?

It is also not helpful that English is being diluted with Spanish being promoted as a second language. A common language gives a nation strength and the modern era is the first where immigrants (legal or illegal) were not encouraged, indeed essentially forced, to adopt English as their national language. We would not be the first society to have dual languages. In ancient Rome at one point there were as many Greek speakers as there were Latin speakers. But that state of affairs descended into anti-Greek sentiment especially among the non-aristocratic classes. A common language encourages other commonalities of interest and strengthens a union of peoples.

At the moment seeking to dissolve the union it is a fringe movement but so were other social movements in their beginning. We need only remember the Nazis to see that what were laughable movements in their beginning turned into something far more serious and far more quickly than most at the time imagined. Ignoring the seeds can only later result in having to deal with a dangerous crop of weeds all too soon.

Chapter 6. Making Peace Possible in Our Time.

2014 is the 100th Anniversary of the start of World War I. Because this war was the start of a series of wars from World War II, the Cold War and the War on Terror this anniversary is a time to consider the future and whether there is a solution to the continuing pattern of warfare or whether it is just part of the human condition. We need to step back and look to see if there is anything that can be done to prevent this continuing sequence of wars or if not prevent them to keep them from spreading into a world war. Those of us who have seen war up close and personal, in my case in Vietnam, know how important it is to avert war. Albert Einstein is quoted as saying that he did not know what would be used in the next world war but he knew that the one after that would be fought with stones. It is not just the pattern of wars but the escalation of violence that is a concern.

Achieving world peace has been a dream for many eons but without much success. Neither the League of Nations nor the United Nations has been successful in preventing wars. Perversely the biggest obstacle to a new world war has been the atomic bomb. Possession of this weapon of mass destruction has backed major powers off from confrontations that could result in its use. The spread of nuclear technology to third world countries, however, could change this state of affairs. And biological warfare adds even a more troubling dimension. In this chapter we will explore what some have thought would be successful in preventing wars and what may yet be successful.

Immanuel Kant in his *Perpetual Peace* in essence proposed strengthening the interdependence of countries and economies as a prescription for peace. A promoter of republican government, freedom of travel between states and formation of a league of nations his is a thoughtful overview of causes and potential solutions. He also proposed abolishing standing armies but as we learned in the lead up to World War II that solution adopted after World War I did not deter German aggression. Indeed the Allied countries had a difficult time of playing catch up once the threat emerged. However many of Kant's points are valid and his essential idea was that if a country had more to lose than to gain by going to war it will be held back from war. The concept of MAD (an accurate acronym if there ever was one!) of Mutual Assured Destruction during the Cold War was a somewhat perverse example where each side was deterred from use of nuclear weapons by the assurance that the response would be overwhelmingly devastating. While intertwined and mutual interests and the risk of loss exceeding gain may be effective as a safeguard for rational governments those controlled by religious, tribal or ideological fervor are not likely to find economic ties or economic loss sufficient to prevent their advancing what they see as their destiny via a war.

So let's first consider the basic underlying causes of war. First is a form of greed. The desire to capture lands and peoples and milk them of their resources for the benefit of the warring nation. Whether it is seeking territory or resources or both. In this chapter we will call this cause the Economic Cause of war. Second is religion. Today we see the rise of terrorism, a form of warfare, arising out of the Muslim world. But over the centuries we have seen more than a few wars fought over religious principle. In Africa we see numerous tribal wars which are perhaps a subset of the religious cause. We will call these causes of war the Religious Cause of war. Another cause of war is pressure from within a country causing its leadership to seek outside wars to take away internal pressures. This cause of war might be called the Internal Pressure Cause of war. Then there is what I will call the Accidental Cause of war. A miscalculation on the part of one country that results in a confrontation and some spark that sets off a more general conflict. Finally there is the Ideological War. This may have aspects of the Economic or Religious Causes. The Civil War in the United States may be the best example of an Ideological War whether you ascribe the causes to be anti-slavery vs. pro slavery or you view it is an expression of states' rights and right of secession.

So we are looking at five major causes of potential warfare each of which needs to be addressed separately. These are:

Economic Causes

Religious Causes

Internal Pressure Causes

Accidental Causes

Ideological Causes

Of these causes of war the Religious or Ideological Causes are perhaps the most difficult to deal with. The Accidental Cause may well benefit from intervention by the United Nations or a coalition of nations to defuse situations that could be trigger points for more general warfare. Economic causes are perhaps more easily addressed. None, of course, is easy to address but some are more difficult than others. And while general demilitarization is not likely to prevent war the presence of a military industrial complex such as General (and later President) Eisenhower warned about is always a source of potential destabilization.

One underlying cause for concern is the continued rise of population in the world. A rise which has increased population exponentially. The problems of population growth are increasing at what can only be viewed as an alarming rate.

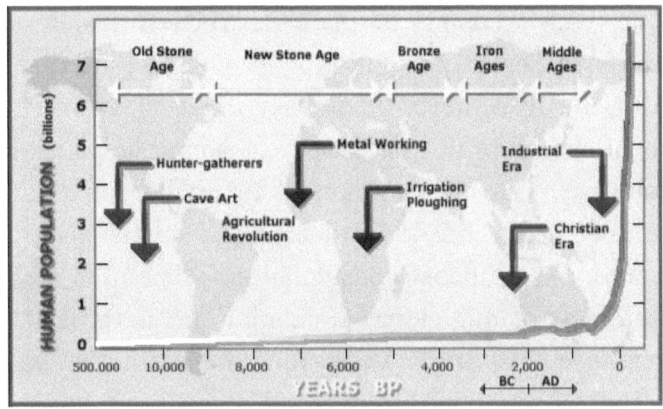

Source: University of Michigan

Despite China and its one child policy, the only nation to attempt a solution, we face a world where we see a continued rise in population that is a strain on resources, a cause of environmental damage and an increasing pressure on governments around the world. Those who would argue this is not a real issue point to Malthus, an economist who predicted two centuries ago that population would outstrip resources. But the fact that it has not played out exactly as Malthus predicted does not mean that massive increases in population are not potential time bombs for the global community. John Maynard Keynes listed this as one of his primary worries. He is not alone.

If there is one step that the world can take to lessen the risk of global conflict it is to promote population control and to begin to reverse the path of doubling population every generation or two. Absent a natural phenomenon like the Black Death or other illness spreading and wiping out large segments of population or damage to the environment that results in mass starvation and death or war with weapons of mass destruction also resulting in massive deaths prevention of population increase will be difficult to achieve. It is easy to see how overloading a boat can cause disaster but overloading the planet is not so obvious. One does not have to favor abortion as alternative or not honor life if birth control itself is made a major focus. A secondary consideration is that often the best and brightest of our global population are those less likely to produce offspring. And a further issue is that as we find ways of extending life expectancy this too puts pressure on population of the planet. One does not have to adopt a eugenics approach to find all of this a concern.

Economic Causes can come in many forms. Probably the best known are the hyperinflation caused in Germany as a result of French invasion of the Ruhr to collect their war reparations from World War I. There is little doubt that this disruption added fuel to the fire that ultimately resulted in Hitler's rise to power and World War II. Taxation by Great Britain was a chief factor in the US revolution and economic conditions in France resulted in the beheading of their king and queen and their Revolution. Japan's entry into World War II was precipitated in large part by their fear of being cut off from what were for them vital supplies of oil and other natural resources. Our recent wars in Iraq were the result of pressure on oil supplies and risk to further disruptions of oil production in the Gulf region. What is instructive in all of these situations is that economic pressures can be the flashpoint for war. Preventing these wars requires careful and early attention to emerging economic problems. Failure to address economic issues before they reach flashpoints can give fuel to those, like Hitler, who would feed on economic distress to achieve political power.

Which brings us back to the problem of population control. Unless the world is able to control growth in population the hope of preventing economic disruption in the future is doomed to failure. Not only does increasing population put pressure on resources it can result in a greater and greater disparity of wealth that in turn can lead to social unrest and ultimately to war. Those focused on trying to spread the wealth due to income inequality unfortunately are also doomed to failure. A recent article indicated that the 85 wealthiest people in the world own more wealth than half the population of the earth. I have no idea if that is true or not but even if it is and you took all that wealth and spread it across the population of the world it would be like pouring a bucket of water in the ocean. Instead of raising standards of living you are likely only to stifle innovation and take away any incentive for work and advancement leaving only the poor (and the corrupt) in the world. The creation of billionaires while middle class population declines is obviously a matter of concern as is the influence of the super rich in global politics. But to attack those who have accumulated wealth legitimately is not a solution. At least one part of a solution is to control population. Without such control of population whatever efforts we make to provide for economic advancement is building sand castles in the way of a rising tide.

Turning to Religious Causes this is the hardest and most difficult to solve. Whether it be the Reformation and Counter Reformation of the Middle Ages, the persecution of Christians in the Roman era or the Islamic terror issue today when faced with those fired with religious fervor who believe violence is justified by their religion once this has taken hold it is likely beyond control. And the biggest problem is that religion relies on faith not reason. We have seen in the United States example after example of hucksters claiming to be religious ministers milking people out of their savings for their religious causes. After all who can refute the claim that God has come to them and given them divine guidance? Disproving religious claims is impossible. Likewise the twisting of religious texts be it the Bible or the Koran or other religious document to fit an agenda is easily achieved. Islamic radicals claim the Koran justifies their war on infidels while virtually every army from the earliest days has claimed that God (or gods in the case of those not monotheistic) is on their side.

So what, if anything, can be done to prevent religion from erupting into war? Recognition of the issue is the first step. Then the marshaling of global leadership to rally those among religious groups who are moderate is a second step. Creation of a culture of religious tolerance is a third step. Probably the best hope is the spread of globalization as it brings cultures and religions together where exposure to different cultures and religions may help to increase religious tolerance. Not among the most rabid but among the general population. Where there is no exposure to other cultures or religions there is an insularity that allows for prejudices in favor of whatever the local religion. Not that there cannot be conflicts where religions come into contact with one another but there is more hope for development of tolerance where there is religious diversity. At the moment the United States is probably the most diverse religious nation in the world. How that diversity ultimately plays out will tell us a lot about whether this diversity leads to tolerance or intolerance. Only by early identification and action is it possible to try and prevent the rise of a religious war. And those who actively promote such wars are quick to seize on economic distress to justify their actions, so eliminating economic distress is a major goal.

Internal Pressure Causes can arise from any number of sources. Economic pressure is obviously a factor in many of these wars. When faced with internal revolt projecting outward has been the answer for many countries. Germany in World War II is probably the greatest recent example. Rallying a population against a perceived (or created) external threat is always a way for a government under pressure to seek to relieve that pressure. Again, recognition early of a rise in such pressures may be the only way to seek to resolve them before they erupt into war.

Accidental Causes are usually the result of miscalculation of the response of an opponent or an incident that inflames the population of a country. Or these causes can simply be the final straw in a building potential conflict as with the death of the Archduke that began a series of dominos that resulted in World War I. Or Germany thinking that France and Great Britain would not declare war after the invasion of Poland. Or thinking that the world would not step in after the Iraqi invasion of Kuwait. Once more only by addressing rising issues before they reach a flashpoint can there be hope of preventing Accidental Causes from erupting into more general war.

And finally there are Ideological Causes. Whether these are wars of liberation or wars resulting from social and economic beliefs such as National Socialism in Germany, Communism in Russia and China these causes are similar to Religious Causes. Only by early identification and counter action can there be hope for prevention of wars arising from ideology.

Recognition of these causes of war is the first step to their prevention. Can all wars be prevented? Probably not. But there are steps we can take to try and prevent limited wars from spreading into global conflict. First is to engender in the global population an understanding and a willingness to act to prevent wars. The League of Nations and United Nations had promise but they have generally failed in preventing wars. That does not mean they do not have a place in seeking a solution. Perhaps the biggest hope for long term peace is the increasing globalization of economies where more and more nations have more to lose by engaging in war than they have to gain. Companies stretching around the globe have a part in identifying and defusing potential for war. And as globalization results in more and more interaction of peoples of different backgrounds, religious and ideological beliefs there is a hope for more and more understanding of others and tolerance of their viewpoints. One can hope that this can lead to a commonality of interest and an increase in tolerance. But all of this is hopeless without population control. Anyone who has looked at the chart of long term population growth can only be alarmed at the rate of increase and its potential for long term global discord and disaster.

Concluding Thoughts

Is achieving peace and prosperity in the global community possible? Is it likely? Unfortunately it would appear that while it is possible that it is increasingly unlikely. That does not mean that those concerned with these issues should simply give up and stop trying to find solutions. The old saying that a journey of a thousand miles begins with the first step applies to dealing with these issues as well. Only by trying to find solutions and building on solutions that are found to work will we have hope for the future of our generation and generations to come.

There is a great danger too in trying to project into the future and solve future problems that may or may not come to pass. Malthus and his prediction that population growth would outstrip global resources has yet to prove true. The Club of Rome made a similar prediction in the 1970's as to oil and other natural resources. They too failed in their attempt to accurately predict the future. So in our attempt to achieve perpetual peace and prosperity we must be wary of those who claim to be able to predict the future. Even global population growth, troubling as it is, may one day see a radical reversal due to any number of causes. Hopefully those causes will be those less drastic than world pandemic or war or global environmental changes resulting in famine.

Each of us has the potential to be part of the global solution by increasing our tolerance of others and our understanding of issues that can lead to both economic and military turmoil. Increasing civility and compassion and once again striving for advancement of the best and the brightest among our population to position of leadership in economic, scientific and political realms. And turning away from and exposing those who would drive wedges between people, be it on economic, racial, religious or ideological grounds. We have seen too often in the last century where this path leads. May we be successful in avoiding these paths as we move into the decades ahead.

www.ingramcontent.com/pod-product-compliance
Lightning Source LLC
Chambersburg PA
CBHW050518290526
45786CB00007B/2618